ISBN 978-1-4477-9429-5

Dedication

Bob and Lilian Dockerty

This book is dedicated to the following:

Robert Daniel Dockerty (Dad).
Lilian Dockerty (Mum).

Sadly no longer with us, but without them, I would not be here and neither would this book!

The Author

Chris Dockerty was born in Germany in September 1959, the son of a serving soldier. He is the third of three sons and the brother of three sisters. Chris moved back to the UK when he was six months old and resided in the North East of England with his family.

In 1970 Chris went to Military Boarding School in Dover, where he grew to be independent and gained a great sense of humour. He was a keen rugby player and turned down a trial for Northumberland Juniors to take up a career in the armed forces. He continued in his sport whilst serving and studied to be an electronics engineer. Upon leaving the forces he has worked in the electrical industry and with local communities as well as becoming a karaoke host and entertainer with a love of music.

He has a keen interest in the local history and family history and always striving to improve his life and that of everyone else around him. He has written this book based on the experience he has gained during his life, and took a tongue in cheek attitude towards everything.

"There are no such things as problems! Only, solutions"

Prologue

This book is written to take a look at my past experiences in a light hearted way, I can only apologise for any coincidental likenesses to anyone I met during my life whose traits may show up here. You may recognise yourself in some of the characters portrayed, but this is not meant intentionally. You must learn to laugh at yourself, as I do, or there would be no sense of humour left in this world.

The purpose of this book is to take you on a journey through life and to explain what it was like and the changes that have taken place up to now. These views are from the point of view of the author and should not be taken literally, because everyone has their own way of seeing how things were then and are now.

Rambling through the countryside you get your hills and valleys, just as you ramble through life there are highs and lows, so let me now ramble on about my life!

All I expect any reader to do is enjoy this book and make up their own mind.

Chris Dockerty

Chapter 1

In The Beginning

This is basically when my life started and I had something to ramble on about. This photo shows Kevin my first friend and me outside his dad's garage in Throckley.

Don't be fooled by the cute appearances!

That is not a lightning bolt going through us in the picture, it is a crease in the old photograph!

In The Beginning

My journey begins at a hospital in Germany on the second of September 1959, my mum was taken to hospital to give birth to her third son, me! If you think this was bad enough, imagine how I felt. I was in a foreign country about to be born, firstly I had the language barrier to cross. How could I possibly understand the German language, after all I was the son of English parents. Then there was, the cultural differences like not being allowed to hang the washing out on a Sunday, how would my mother cope with the dirty nappies?

As it turned out I seem to have been the first Iron Man, this is because, when I was born I took most of the iron from my mothers' blood, this caused her to be detained in hospital for a good few weeks after giving birth to me. I nearly killed her, this greatly reduced my popularity from the start. I would have to make up for this in later life I told myself at the time.

Once my mother came out of hospital, my two older brothers and me seemed to enjoy the rest of the next six months in Germany, visiting the Black Forest, home of the famous German cake, where I remember seeing photos of us all there together, however, there was one disturbing picture of me alone and abandoned in the middle of this great forest. Perhaps they decided to leave me there! I don't know, whatever happened, they must have changed their minds, because at the six month stage, we all returned to England and moved to a little village called Millfield in the North East of the country on the outer west of Newcastle upon Tyne.

Then came a big surprise, one year, one month and two days after my birth, my mother gave birth to our first sister. I guessed that was it for me as there was seven years between my oldest brother and me, then four years between me and my other brother. That's right, three sons then along came a daughter, what chance had we now, the only girl in the family! I was the youngest so I guess I had to try harder to be noticed, at least my brothers had a little bit of experience in life.

So there was I at the tender age of one year, one month and two days now with a young sister with whom I would have to fight to get my hands on the last of the baby rusks. How was I to cope? As it happens I didn't do too badly, my parents treat us as equals after putting my sister first. I think that it was at this early stage I learnt very quickly how to look after myself and work to get what I wanted. So my first sister probably came as a blessing as far as I'm concerned. I had no chance of becoming a spoilt brat.

It was about this time in my life I realised that there was another woman living with us, this turned out to be my mothers' mum, in other words my grandmother. She was a very religious woman and took great pride in looking after us all, although sometimes I think that she did not always approve of my dad, but hey! Isn't that what mother in laws are meant to be like.

We lived here like this as a family until I was about three or four years old, then we moved up to another part of the area known as Throckley. My most vivid memory about this move was the fact that it took place in winter. While my two brothers were at school, my mum walked us the mile up the road to our new home in the snow. I know it was snowing because of the copious amount of snow I gathered in my wellington boots, I am sure my sister got let off lightly from this freezing white stuff as she was pushed all the way in her pushchair, leaving me to suffer the possibility of frostbite and exposure.

Throckley I found to be an exciting adventure compared to where we had been living. We lived in what was known as the white city, not because of the snow, but because all the houses were painted white. We lived in a street which had a steep incline to it, and opposite our house was a square of old peoples bungalows surrounding a park like area. This was great as we now had a space to play and hang about. This was where I met my first good friend Kevin, who lived at the top of our street and was only one year older than me. George his older brother also became friends with my brother Bobby. At this stage, my sister Christine had no female friends so spent most of her time hanging about with me and Kevin.

The fact that Christine had no real girls at the time to play with, mum enrolled her in dancing lessons with a dance teacher called Olwyn Brown, not only this, after realising my sister never had a dance partner, mum enrolled me in the lessons as well. This was where I was taught Ballroom and Latin American dancing. We were entered into competitions, which I don't think we ever won, but I think it was because my mother liked to see Christine in her sequin dance dresses and me in black trousers, white shirt and dickie bow tie. We passed exams in dancing and were certified for it. This was the start of getting roped into doing things with my sister. The dancing bit was getting to be too much. Mum had us practising in the house every chance she got. No wonder I spent most of my time out with my friends.

Another thing I remember is the fact that my parents bought us clothes to get dressed up in like cowboy and Indian sets, dad liked his western films. Did anyone notice that in these films, the cowboys always won. I bet that was why they bought Christine a cowgirl outfit and me an Indian one. I liked watching Captain Scarlett on TV and wanted to get his outfit, but what did I end up with? A thunderbirds costume, I have been dressed as Batman without a robin, a knight and a roman centurion in the school nativity plays. I had no chance!

It was at this point that I began to enjoy my life we would collect wild bees in jam jars to keep as pets from the bush at the top of the street, this bush is still there to this day, collect snails to race against each other and keep fit by playing knock nine doors, much to the annoyance of the old people in the bungalows. At the back of our house we had a garden where my father would grow his own vegetables, also in this garden there was a little area where we were allowed to play. I spent a lot of time here playing with my toy soldiers and cars, and it was here I discovered two ants nests, one with red ants and one with black ants. These ant nests gave me an idea, plastic soldiers fighting each other was not as exciting as seeing a real war, so I introduced the ants to each other and watched as they fought for supremacy invading each others nests. My keen interest in wildlife had begun. It was a miracle that we never seemed to get stung from the bees or ants and our mothers got sick of getting complaints from the neighbours and taking snails out of our trouser pockets. But try as we might we never failed to get reprimanded by our parents at least once a week, if we didn't, then there was something wrong or by some miracle we never got caught. Another of the local favourite games I learned while living in this area was hide and seek, the only problem I found was that, whenever I was on, that is I had to look for everyone, I could never find them. Maybe it was their way of getting away from me!

Mum and dad took us camping for a week nearly every year for our holidays. One year, both myself and Bobby got tents for Christmas and we wanted to take these with us, Bobby's was better than mine as he had a sewn in groundsheet. Mine was canvass with wooden poles. We were taken to Cullercoats this year, and we all pitched our tents, Bobby was sleeping in his and I was going to sleep in mine. Dad took us to the beach one evening, he could have picked a better one as it was raining, but never the less it was exciting. We sat at the top of the cliffs and watched the beach as seals started to come ashore, we were fascinated. When we walked back to the camp site, the rain got heavier, so we all retired to our tents for the night. Next morning, I woke up soaked and it seemed that my tent had shrunk, one end was lying on my head and the other end on my feet, being young at the time, I was very upset. I got up and told mum and dad, when they came out, they noticed that someone had stolen my guy ropes and caused the tent to collapse. We searched high and low for these ropes, but could not find them. I refused to stay in the tent anymore, but the funny thing was, Bobby walked about with a mischievous smile on his face for the rest of the holiday, but I could not prove he was to blame.

As time went on my two brothers, Steve and Bobby, and I started getting models and little soldiers. We used to build the models, these were mostly tanks, armoured cars and aeroplanes and the soldiers were replicas of armies from the Second World War like American marines, British paratroopers, Japanese soldiers and German soldiers. Once we had amassed our armies, we had war games in our bedroom, these sometimes ended in real battles between us. Steve was a teenager in his final years at school and would shortly leave and start his apprenticeship as an electrician at Throckley Brick Works. Bobby was still at school and still fighting while he was there. Steve had also started playing guitar and, I must say, he was good at it. Other things I remember about the things we used to play with were an electric train set, the transformer was used by Steve once to wire up Bobby and my metal bunk beds, luckily Bobby was on the top bunk and as he had to make contact with both beds at the same time was the only one to get an electric shock, which Steve and me found highly amusing. We had electric racing cars, but I kept crashing and Leggo building bricks, and Meccano to encourage us into the building trade.

Mum and dad enjoyed their well earned nights out at the local social club at the weekends, often leaving my two brothers, Christine and myself to babysit each other. On one occasion, Christine and I were playing a board game, when for some unknown reason Christine put the dice up her nose, where it got stuck. After trying to get it out for ages, mum and dad returned home to discover this situation. On trying to remove the dice, it had been pushed further up the nostril. Dad took her to the hospital to have it removed and when he returned with our distressed sister, he proudly announced that she had thrown a six.

When I was about eight years old and it was getting near to Christmas, mum was in hospital again giving birth to our second sister, Fiona. More problems, where were we all going to stop, there was now five kids. The problem was solved a couple of years later when we moved back to Newburn. The new house had three storeys and was on the main road.

Steve being the oldest and a teenager by now did not like having to be in at the same time as his two younger brothers, so he developed a technique of climbing out of the bedroom window, down the drainpipe onto the outhouse roof and away to see his friends. This was copied by Bobby a little later on. I found that my older brothers found a lot more time to argue and fight with each other on a regular basis. This was something I would also end up doing later on in my life. Although we fought, we always covered each others backs. There was once when Bobby was in the army, but had come home on leave for a couple of weeks, Steve and Bobby started arguing in the bedroom which we all shared, this got more and more out of control until Bobby picked up one of his army boots, which was studded and threw it at our Steve across the room. Steve saw it coming and ducked down. The boot then flew past his head and went out of the window, breaking it on the way through. Realising what had been going on, they both dived into bed and pretended to be asleep as our dad came up the stairs asking what was going on with the offending boot in his hand. They both denied fighting and told him that they had been asleep, but when they noticed the boot, they soon changed their minds and were punished as well as having to pay for a new window.

One Christmas I was given a dartboard, which I played with in our bedroom and one day Bobby came in and decided to get in the way of the board every time I wanted to play, I got more and more frustrated at this and eventually lost my temper. I threw the dart while he was in the way and it stuck in his head, he looked like a Dalek from Doctor Who. Bobby then took the dart from his head when he realised what I had done, grabbed me by the hair and proceeded to put my head in the door and repeatedly slammed the door shut on it. We were making a lot of noise, alerting mum who started to shout up the stairs to ask what we were doing to which we both replied in unison, nothing! She never came up to investigate and I'm sure she never knew about this incident.

Grandma was still living with us dad worked hard to keep the pennies rolling in and mum worked and cooked to keep everyone happy. I remember the old flat roofed outhouse attached to the house which was used as a wash room with an old boiler washing machine and a mangle. Dad often used it as a workshop to make toys for us out of wood. So for one Christmas I got a wooden fort made out of wood along with cowboy and Indian figures to play with and my sister Christine got a wooden dolls house with all the wooden furniture and little electric lights to go with it.

The sixties in Throckley was a strange time, there were mods and rockers, and out of the back of our house were the flats. It was in the car parks amongst these flats that another, what seemed a stranger group of people met on their motorbikes, these were the local Hells Angels. They had souped up bikes with long handle bars and they all dressed up in leather clothes which were decorated with unusual designs, but to top all this, they wore strange helmets like German army ones, I thought at times we had been invaded again. Dad had a Triumph Herald car, which was once parked further up the street at the top of a hill beside where his council garage was. One day, Kevin, me and Bobby were hanging about his car, which was open, pretending to drive it, when Bobby left, me and Kevin decided to stay a bit longer. I found this lever in the car and being clever, not knowing what it was, let it off. I panicked when the car started to move and jumped out. The car rolled down the hill and luckily stopped at the bottom without hitting anything. Dad was furious when he found out someone had moved his car without him knowing. He never found out that it was us.

Time soon started to fly past after our move to Throckley, and it wasn't long before my fifth birthday came up. On my fifth birthday I got the surprise of my life, horror of horrors, I started school! What a day to start school, actually on your birthday. I must have wondered what other nasty things were to take place during my life, as if starting school wasn't bad enough, the school I was to attend was Newburn Manor County Primary, right next to Millfield, where we lived before our move to Throckley.

Chapter 2

Schooldays

Starting school on my fifth birthday was bad enough, never mind the school photographs.

This stage of my life takes us through starting school to taking my first exams, starting with the eleven plus exam which you will get the results to later on in this chapter. Not to mention the other exams I took to get to boarding school.

That's me in the middle row third from the left.

Schooldays

It was strange starting school this was the first time that I had got out of bed on my birthday, had breakfast, opened my presents, then was whisked out of the door, the same time as my brothers and back to Newburn to this strange institution. I thought I was going on a special birthday trip, as it turned out it was in a way, my first trip to school. My mother took me in and spoke to some grown ups while I was stood there in a confused state trying to work out where all these other kids were coming from. Were we being left here because our parents couldn't cope or were sick of us? The questions running through my head were ridiculous. As it turned out it was the place where I was meant to start something called my education! As if I knew what education was at that age! Then my mother went home and left me to get on with it.

There seemed to be loads of us, in my class there were four Helens, two Alans, two Stephens, a Charlie, a Geoff, a Reuben and a Colin to name but a few. I was wondering whether to give numbers to the Helens, Stephens and Alans to tell them apart, then I discovered that they had last names as well. At this early stage of my education, we seemed to play a lot occasionally interrupted by the grown ups to draw, read, write and do things with numbers which I later discovered was called mathematics.

During our breaks the boys all played football which was alright unless you fell over or were pushed over because the playground was concrete surrounded by solid stone walls. The girls seemed to play something called hopscotch and ring a ring of roses. I knew that my friend Kevin was at school, but I never seemed to get to see him, he was always with these other friends of his, so we used to hang about when we got home. Playing football was great at this stage, even though I was always the one in goal, perhaps this was so the other lads could kick the ball at me as hard as they could, or cause me to dive to save the ball and land on the hard concrete surface grazing my knees and injuring myself in other ways.

The one problem I had here was my broad Geordie accent which the teachers tried their hardest to make me lose I couldn't understand their problem with it because I could understand myself.
Whenever I told them," Am gannin yem."
They would say, "No Christopher. It's not 'am gannin yem', it's I am going home."

I often wish that they would go home and stop bugging me and trying to make me talk posh. This went on all through my time at Newburn School, but the teachers had no success in stopping my accent. They even told my mother about my accent telling her that I was hard to understand at times. Being born in Germany, I wondered what they would do if I spoke in German to them all the time.

While I was at this school, I discovered that I had this annoying skin problem called eczema which caused me to itch all the time, so I was forever scratching, the other kids must have thought I had the plague or something. It was particularly bad in the winter when it snowed. For fun we used to have snowball fights and scrub each other in the snow, the adverse effects to this, was my eczema broke out and I was covered in sores. Great, what else could possibly go wrong with me at this stage of my life? Where shall I begin, oh yes, while here I got both types of measles, the mumps, my teeth were overcrowding my mouth, so mum took me to the dentist to have a few removed and a brace fitted and I was forever getting teased about being born in Germany. I was suddenly a Nazi who loved Hitler and no one could understand how I was actually English. That's kids for you. Between nineteen sixty four and nineteen seventy, no one told the kids at Newburn School that the second world war finished in nineteen forty five.

Having told you that there were negatives, a lot of my time at this school held good memories. It was while I was here I became a keen football player, but instead of my parents buying me a Newcastle football strip, they bought me an England one. I had my first guitar lesson here where I learned to play Kumbaya my lord, once I learnt this tune I thought I was a rock star even though it was a boy scouts camp fire song. Talking about the boy scouts, when we were young, Kevin and me both went to join the local group, but were kicked out on the night we joined much to the disgust of our parents, we were older by now and still on a roll of getting told off by our parents. On the football side of things, me and my classmates all took pride in being on the school team, even though we never played other schools. We only played against ourselves on the sports afternoon which happened to be every Wednesday. This took place on the school field which was on an incline, had a crater on it, a big bald patch in the middle and no goal posts. I remember on one occasion during the hot weather, I was in goal when I saw a large black cloud heading our way. The strange thing about this cloud was the fact that it was approaching very quickly and at head height, it was only when the teacher started shouting at us all to get down or run did we realise that this was no ordinary cloud, in fact it was the biggest swarm of bees that I have ever seen. The only thing I remember about that match after it was abandoned was the score. Football teams twenty two, bees twenty thousand. We lost!

Swimming lessons were also a positive part of being with this school. We were taught to swim at Newburn Pool which was situated at West Denton, causing more confusion to my young brain. The school took us there weekly to swim, I started swimming like a brick at first, wondering how some of the kids in my class could already stay afloat and move in the water. Eventually I got the hang of it and by the time I left the school, I had gained my Bronze life saving swimming certificate and medal. For this I had to dive to the bottom of the deep end to retrieve a brick, I thought at the time that the brick was me when I first started to swim.

One other thing that we all learned at Newburn was how to fight. Fights were well organised so they happened after school and the venue was always the school field, where we played football. Fights were a regular occurrence and they were arranged by someone having a bad day or having a silly argument during school hours with someone else. Another way would be someone saying that one person was tougher than another, so they goaded the two into having a fight to settle their curiosity. I must admit that I was not much of a one to go for a fight, except to watch and cheer my friends on who were chosen to fight that week, but somehow I still managed to get roped into a fight every now and then. The strange thing with the teachers was that even though they always seemed to know when a fight was going to take place, they always turned up near the end to break up the cheering crowds of kids that formed a circle around the fighters. Dad didn't help much either, I remember coming home with a black eye after one fight, my dad noticed it and asked if I won when he realised I had been fighting. When I told him no, he threatened to beat me if I lost my next one, so I got no sympathy there. One fight I do remember was with one of my best friends at the school, to this day I cannot work out why it happened in the first place. I was going home from school on an ordinary day when a crowd from the school started following me, calling me a coward for not fighting this person. We had not been arguing and got on well together, but the crowd just kept on at me so I lost my temper and went to confront my friend. We ended up fighting for what seemed a lifetime, wearing each other out. The crowd were all shouting support for my opponent, after us punching and kicking each other for about five to ten minutes, we were both worn out and we thought we would call it a draw. No chance! The crowd pushed us on to continue fighting until one of us won, both of us absolutely shattered continued, then I got a lucky punch in and winded him. The fight was over and I won, but instead of the usual well done to me and hard luck to my opponent, I was bombarded with comments like, dirty fighter and coward. I gave up, picked up my coat and went home. I couldn't win a black eye in a fight that day. The following day both my opponent and I were good friends again.

One plus with this schooling lark was that we had school trips if our parents could afford them. My first ever school trip was to Edinburgh Zoo. I remember going to school early, getting herded onto a coach by the teachers for the long journey to Scotland. When we arrived, we were guided into the zoo where the first thing to grab my attention was the polar bears in an enclosure near the entrance. I was fascinated by them and all the other animals I saw there, including the elephants, penguins, tigers, lions and monkeys. The monkeys reminded me of some of my friends at the time. I took pocket money with me kindly donated by my mum and dad. This money I spent on presents for them, I bought them a porcelain elephant and bought myself a few plastic ape and gorilla figures. The trip lasted all day and upon my return home I was absolutely shattered. That elephant reminded me of that trip for years to come.

Christmas was always a strange time at this school, every year they would put on a nativity play for our parents. I however was never chosen to play Joseph or one of the wise men or kings, no! I was always picked to play the roman centurion sent to kill the baby Jesus. Was it my dad's military background, or was I being trained for my later life, I didn't know at the time, it's just the war games at home, my dad being in the army and by this time training army cadets and the fights at school, was I meant to be a violent person or just being trained in case? My later schooling would not improve my thoughts about this. The problem with these nativity plays and me were the fact that no matter how small my part was I suffered from stage fright to the extent of losing my voice and sore throats. Not that any of this mattered, because they had still not managed to get me to lose my Geordie accent, so if I did speak no one would understand me anyway.

As my time continued through this school, I became the chief prefect at the tender age of eleven. My reading and writing skills improved, I felt I was quite good at art, but I hated maths and ended up taking extra lessons to catch up, but it was either because I had a Geordie accent and couldn't understand it or the maths teacher was useless. The maths teacher had no sense of humour and seemed to be beating the lessons into the pupils. Hence my start in the world of mathematics was flawed from the start. I had to do more work myself to improve my education, after all my eleven plus examination was drawing ever nearer. The eleven plus exam was designed to decide whether pupils from our school and other schools like us went to the grammar school or the secondary school. Grammar schools were for the brainy and often called snobs while the secondary schools were for the less bright amongst us. It was as I remember a one hour exam covering everything you were taught since starting school. My year was the last year to take this exam before it was abolished. I was determined to pass this exam, just because both my brothers failed it and went to Walbottle West School, one of the secondary schools in the area. As the exam approached, I studied hard determined to pass, when the exam day came. I was poised and prepared, new pencil and rubber at the ready, nothing was going to stop me. I opened the paper when told and started to read. Nothing was going in, how was I meant to remember the answer to this and that questions? I was taught that, years earlier. Writing away steadily, my confidence was building, if I did well on everything else, then the mathematics part wouldn't let me down too much. Finally the hour was up after what seemed to be five minutes, the teacher told us to stop writing and put our pencils down. But I still had questions from the sheet that needed answering. Walking out of the room I told myself that the exam wasn't that hard, but not sure if that was true. Meanwhile my parents had been toying with the idea of boarding school, why I do not know, neither of my brothers went, maybe if I passed then I wouldn't have to go either. Time passed by and soon the results of the eleven plus exam came, eagerly I awaited my results, did I pass or fail? The answer came all too soon, I failed miserably. Resigned to the fact that I would have to follow my brothers into secondary school, I decided to look into the boarding school prospect with my parents. Time was short and decisions had to be made.

Questions to be asked were. Where is the school and is it really that bad? The answers are the school was in Dover and it wasn't really that bad. The main problem was now I had to go through two further exams and an interview. The exams were sent to Newburn and then I had to travel to Dover with my dad for the interview. The other thing I didn't realise before I took the exams was that this school was a Military Boarding School. So while everyone else at Newburn School carried on with their normal lessons I was isolated in a classroom twice for separate two hour long exams which I thought were more difficult than the eleven plus, but surprise, surprise I passed both entrance exams and was accepted into the school. Next step was the interview.

Chapter 3

Boarding School Days

This is dad, Fiona, sister number two and me at my Boarding School. The Duke of Yorks Royal Military School in Dover.

I knew there was a plan to get me into uniform.

Boarding School Days

The big day of the interview at my new boarding school was fast approaching. Dad had our tickets for the journey to Dover from Newcastle, overnight bags were packed and we were on our way. This was a big adventure to me, catching the bus to the railway station and getting on the train. Upon arrival at Newcastle station, dad decided to buy something to read on the journey, he also bought something for me to do on the long journey, to stop me getting bored. Finally we were on the platform and this big old diesel train pulled up, it had come from Edinburgh, the zoo town and was going to a station in London called Kings Cross. I wasn't quite sure why it was stopping in London, but dad put me right by telling me we had to change trains there. I thought it was because it would have run out of fuel by the time we arrived. I was taking everything in, because I knew that I would have to do this journey a lot more times by myself. This journey was before the invention of the faster 125 train, and took about, what seemed a lifetime, six hours. The journey was boring, especially when it kept stopping at several stations to pick up other passengers. I was shattered when it finally arrived at Kings Cross. Glad to get off the train and stretch my legs, we headed for a taxi, I noticed that there were a few more boys with parents, and they all seemed to be going in the same direction as us.

The taxi dropped us off at Charing Cross station, where we had to catch our second train. I looked at this second train in horror, it was like the ones from the black and white movies that dad watched, it had separate compartments which only sat about six to eight people. During this second train trip, dad fell asleep, I knew this from the snoring noises coming from him. Eventually, we arrived at Dover about Six o Clock in the evening, where we were greeted by some adults who were checking off names and ushering us onto buses. I was beginning to think that we would never reach this new school I was going to. I did notice though that several of the boys I saw in London and their parents were also getting on these buses, so they must be going to the same school as me. Eventually we arrived after driving past Dover Castle, up this hill into what seemed another world. I had never seen a school as big as this one. We were greeted, then shown where we were sleeping, this was good for me as I was worn out and needed to sleep, anyway tomorrow was a big day.

Next morning we were woken up early, got washed and dressed, then were taken to breakfast in this large old hall. It seemed deserted apart from us fresh visitors. This was followed by a tour of the school, after this we had to attend a briefing about the school, followed by our interviews. During the initial tour of the school, dad met one of his old army buddies that he had served with and started talking. They both were so engrossed in catching up with each other that they forgot about their sons, namely Trevor and me. They were so busy talking that we lost sight of everyone else as they disappeared into one of the doors of the education block. All these doors looked the same, so we didn't know where they had all gone. Then dad realised that we were alone with his friend and Trevor, he asked where everyone went. I told him they went to the briefing in one of the classrooms, he looked horrified as he didn't know which classroom, remember, we had never been here before. Dad's friend asked what we were going to do, I calmly told them to follow me. They looked confused, but followed me anyway. I led them through a door, along a couple of corridors and straight to the classroom where everyone was waiting. Dad asked me how I knew where to go, so I told him I had been there before, he replied that we had never been there before. This made me feel dizzy and strange, because I was convinced I had been there before, in fact I had actually been there with them before. Talk about Déjà vu!

After the briefing, I had my interview, where I told them that one of my hobbies was doing magic tricks. This had been for a couple of years after getting a magic set one Christmas. The teacher told me to show him one, so I produced a packet of cards from my pocket and showed him a card trick. Yes I still carried loads of stuff in my pockets, but had grown out of the snail stage by now. Dad joked about my interview and the card trick for the rest of his life. I was accepted to go to the school and would start in the new term. All that was left now was to say our goodbyes and continue our long journey home to Newcastle. This was strangest interview I've ever had, but I left them laughing.

My first house at the Duke of York's Royal Military School was Kitchener House this was one of two junior houses. From now on and for the rest of my life I was going to be a Dukie or an Ex Dukie. Dukie is the name given to anyone who attended this school.

Kitchener was a good house and its colours were red, Hague the other junior house had the colour blue. There was fierce competition between these two houses in sports and educational areas, both houses thought theirs was the best. The fierce competitive attitude was instigated by the house tutors, who strove to beat their colleagues in the opposing house. Upon joining this school you also automatically became a member of the C.C.F. (Combined Cadet Force). The school was run in a regimented and disciplined way. Yes it was definitely a military school catering for sons of soldiers, in a way it was probably like national service for kids. This was where I spent the next four years of my life, doesn't time fly when you're enjoying yourself, or kept busy!

A lot of our time while in Kitchener House was spent playing table tennis, doing homework and writing letters home, which was compulsory at least once a week. If we had no letters to write, we had to read a book or carry out another quiet pastime. I read a lot of books during my time here, mostly horror books or joke books, some of which were humorous poems. When we had all been introduced into the art of playing rugby, I was selected to play for the house team. Probably because I could catch a ball, this will be due to all my previous years at school, playing in goal for the football team. I was also selected to play for the school rugby A team from the under elevens until I left the school. We played a lot of sports here.

We had a list of lessons as long as your arm, from English and Mathematics to Latin, French and German, not to mention History, Geography and Physics, my poor brain was overloaded. What was the point in learning Latin? I was hardly going to bump into a Roman Centurion, Latin is a dead language, no one speaks it anymore. It didn't help in my History lessons either, when I was asked where was Hadrians Wall, I replied, "All around Hadrians Garden!" I hated History and Geography and could not get my head around French. German I liked, even though our German teacher looked like Hitler. Every Sunday we all had to get up and go to church in the school chapel. And they held Sunday parades, where we all dressed up in our uniforms and marched around the school parade square. After all we were now members of the combined cadet force, so had to learn how to shoot and live in a field as well as reading a map, Geography again. Then we discovered that the school had a band, so we were all put through a form of audition to see what we might be able to play, and I was selected to learn to play the bugle. My brother Bobby was in the army at this stage and the lead drummer for the Royal Corps of Transport Junior Leaders Corps of Drums. I quite fancied playing the drums myself, but I wasn't allowed to change, so I was stuck with this bugle.

The school did have one good thing, the school tuck shop, this was where we could spend our pocket money on such things as stamps, shoe polish and laces, if we were lucky enough there would be some money left to buy sweets with. Parents were needed at this time, you had to rely on them to send you tuck parcels, a bit like Red Cross parcels they were full of food and little gifts from them. One problem with these was that when you received them and shared them amongst your friends, there was never much left for yourself. Every ten weeks or so we went back home, but after the travelling I had to do I might as well have stayed, because when I got home it felt like it was time to come back to school. I used to bring my bugle home to practise and annoy the neighbours again. I often practised on my old schools' playing field. I lost contact with Kevin and all the friends I started school with, but at last I seemed to have lost my Geordie accent. This I know because everyone started calling me posh.

Stephen my oldest brother was still working at the brick yard and had taken up photography, he built a darkroom in the cupboard in our living room with all the gear to develop and print black and white photographs. I thought this was great and often used the cupboard to hide in. it wasn't long before I was developing and printing my own black and white pictures. I took this hobby back to school with me. Bobby was still in the army busy failing his driving test, not a good thing to be doing in the Royal Corps of Transport, how was he to transport people about? Carry them on his back! Another event while I was at this school was mum gave birth to our third sister, Melanie, she was born seven years after Fiona and fourteen years after Christine which meant I was fifteen years older than her. So the full compliment was three lads and three lasses.

Back at school I concentrated on my sports which consisted of rugby, hockey, athletics, cricket and swimming. Never let anyone tell you hockey is for girls, you will soon change your mind when you have been hit in the face with a hockey ball. Academically, I was put into what they called the technical stream for schoolwork, sounds good to you, but we all knew that it meant decidedly average. Most of us however went onto skilled trade jobs from this stream. Playing rugby was the best for me until one term, on our first practice session after the half term Holidays, I was knocked out and woke up in the schools' medical reception centre, like a mini hospital. I cannot remember to this day what happened, but from what I've been told we were playing against each other after the warm up when I went to tackle one of the lads who was notorious for lifting his knees while running and my head made contact with his knees. I asked if I was found lying there, to which everyone answered no. So when I asked how they knew I was unconscious, they told me that I started playing for the wrong side. I woke up with the biggest headache I've ever had in my life, still in my rugby strip and boots.

Other memories from this school were hanging about on the cliffs at Dover we used to walk down the zig zag, a winding path down the cliff face to the beach which was covered in stones and pebbles, no sand anywhere. We visited the old gun placements here and carried on in the tunnels. On one occasion, there was a landslide and one of our boys got caught in it, I was called on to run up to the school to let them know what had happened while the others dug him out. I ran as hard as I could up to the school almost collapsing on the way, only to discover when I got there that the air sea rescue had been dispatched to help. What amazed me was the fact that no one at the school seemed bothered, I went into the first house to be told that the lad involved was not in that house and to go to his house to report it. Dover castle was another favourite visiting place, but when mum and dad came to visit me one year, mum would not go in because she thought it was haunted. Dad had an old VW camper van at this time and while taking me back to school after my day out, he did an emergency stop and catapulted me from the back of the van to the front of the van. Luckily my face hitting the front seats stopped me from going through the windscreen. It was only Christine and her friend Denise that asked if I was alright. I must have been, I'm here writing about it.

Life went on like this for about four years with me travelling back and forth between Dover and Newcastle for my holidays, then the unthinkable happened. One half term I arrived back in Newcastle Central Station to be met by my oldest brother Steve instead of my mum. He told me that our grandmother was ill and the doctor was at the house, we travelled home on the bus, only to be ushered downstairs and told that she had died. This upset me as she had always been a part of my life and now she was gone. This holiday was spent in misery and finished with her funeral before I returned to the school. It was shortly after this that I came home on holiday and was never to return there again, I was to start going to Walbottle School. This turned out to be a bit of a culture shock to me.

When I started Walbottle, I met up with a few of my friends that I had started school with, but they had changed. I was picked on as being the posh kid, because my accent had changed and my school blazer still had the white rose of York badge on it. I plodded on, skiving off when I could and getting into fights. I played for the school rugby team, but I hated most of my time here. I decided to leave and join the army before taking my exams which went down like a lead weight with the teachers at the school. I remember my last day at school as my day of revenge, if I hadn't already left, I'm sure I would have been thrown out. It was a school sports day and I was still being victimised by some of the lads. I ran the one hundred metres race, then something snapped inside me. I grabbed the first of the bully boys and beat him up, once finished with him I chased another until I caught him and gave him the same treatment. By this time I noticed a crowd beginning to form and follow me, I tracked down another took my anger out on him, then I went after an annoying prefect, who had locked himself inside the school, I managed to get in, but by now the teachers had discovered what was going on, so when I tracked the prefect to a classroom, I opened the door and was about to throw a punch, but stopped myself when I realised that the deputy headmistress was standing in front of me. I told her I was leaving and wished her the best to try and disguise my actions, but she knew what was going on and had me escorted off the school premises. Don't you just love and miss your schooldays?

My next stage in life was joining the army as a Junior Leader in The Royal Electrical and Mechanical Engineers. Just when you thought things couldn't get any worse.

Chapter 4

Basic Training & Apprenticeship

So here we are at the start of my apprenticeship at the Army Apprentices College, Arborfield. This photograph is of the intake 76B taken in 1976.

Junior Company.

I'm front row third from the right.

Basic Training & Apprenticeship

This all started when I was still at school and decided to join the army. I visited the Army Careers Centre in Newcastle upon Tyne and applied to join as an electronics technician after my exams, but after passing the aptitude tests and going through the selection process successfully at Harrogate, I was told that there were no more places left for that intake. I withdrew my application, then after a few weeks decided to apply again for a placement before I took my exams, but they would not accept my previous results, so I had to go through the whole process again. The second time around I was successful again and signed up on the sixth of May 1976. When I was signed up I was sworn in and given a bible at the same time, it was the same bible I was sworn in with.

On May the tenth, my basic training started at Arborfield Army Apprentices College, this was going to be a period in my life that I would remember for a very long time. The college was an army camp made up of wooden buildings with six legs coming from each, these were known as spiders and because they were made of wood, we were informed that they would burn down in a matter of minutes should they catch fire. The new intake block however was a brick building at the head of the parade square, this was known as the junior block where all new Junior Leader Recruits started their lives at the college. Everyone at this college were known as J.E.E.P.S, This stood for Junior Entry Everybody's Personal Slave, the ones who joined straight away as regulars or older recruits were in the neighbouring barracks and were known as Crunchies. The four spiders were where the older junior recruits lived, these were in four companies, namely A, B, C, or D Company. After leaving the junior block, I would end up in B Company.

So there we were all of us new recruits and members of Junior Company. Our first task was, after a short briefing, to get kitted out with our uniforms and get our hair cut. We must have looked a sight, going to the stores, getting asked what size we were and being handed mountains of gear which we had to struggle carrying back to our rooms. I was in a room with seven others, the room next door had another eight of us and these two rooms made up 2 Squad, our squad sergeant and instructor was a sergeant Keeling, a short dark haired bloke, who was also an ex mercenary. He had been serving with his regiment and gained the rank of lieutenant, but got bored with army life and decided to go to Angola as a mercenary for 18 month, but got bored with that, returned to his unit and handed himself in. He was reduced through the ranks, served eighteen month in Colchester military prison, went back to his regiment where he worked his way back to the rank of sergeant and was now here to train us new recruits. I wondered what I was in for, but it wasn't long before I found out. I can't remember who was the worst, him or the two junior or A/T corporals that were nominated to help him train us.

In our first week, we were taught to shave, make beds including bed packs which were later used as a punishment, iron our uniforms the regulation way and bull our boots, this involved using a duster, polish, water and a lot of elbow grease. If they could not see their faces in our boots, we were in trouble. Locker inspections were another regular event with our toothbrushes, razors and everything else being thrown out of windows if they were not considered clean by these NCOs. The room had to be immaculate every day, floors highly polished to the extent we were afraid to walk on them and there was no dust anywhere because they used to check in places even dust had not heard of. Being taught to shave was the strangest because those of us who had no need to shave due to having faces as smooth as a billiard ball still had to shave every morning whether we needed to or not. A lot of the lads suffered from home sickness, something I was cured of due to my time spent at boarding school, but we all got along with one another, covering each others backs and helping one another out. We were marched everywhere and had spot inspections at all hours of the day or night. Changing parades were held if any one of our squad members was picked up on something, these consisted of being told to be on the parade ground in five minutes dressed in PE kit or another one of our uniforms. Once we were on parade in the designated kit, we were told to change and be back in another five minutes dressed in something else, this involved running back to the block, up two flights of stairs, changing and being back on parade within the designated time. This could go on for ages or until the NCOs got bored with their little game. This was normally followed by a half hour break then a locker inspection. Locker inspection! Our kit was all over the place, but we finally got this down to a fine art.

We were taught to drill in a squad and spent hours marching around in circles on the parade square, much to the amusement of the more senior recruits. Even drill was not made easy, the temperatures were in the high seventies and we were in full kit, sweating and trying our hardest not to fall over or pass out in the heat, even swaying a little was frowned upon. On one occasion that I remember, our right hand marker was a bloke called Pitman, he was tall, blonde and broad across the shoulders, towering over the rest of us in the squad. It was on a red hot day and our sergeant had us standing to attention for what seemed a lifetime, when Pitman swayed a little under the heat, sergeant Keeling saw this and immediately lost his temper. He started swearing and cursing, stamping around us and screaming at Pitman, then Keeling swung his pace stick and hit Pitman over the back of his shoulders. The tip of his stick snapped off and landed at his feet. This made him even madder, he stormed around to the front and screamed at us telling us we had just earned an extra hour on the drill square and that Pitman owed him a new stick. The funny thing about this incident was that Pitman never moved after being originally spotted by our sergeant. The weather must have made the sergeant hot under the collar!

Another favourite pastime while we were here was running over the bunkers situated behind our block and walking along the length of ditches full of water during our fitness and tactical training. We regularly visited the gymnasium after long runs so the PE instructors could wear us out or damage us by getting us to free abseil through the roof of the gymnasium, do head-rolls over boxes handsprings over each other or jump up and down on a trampoline after climbing long ropes to the gymnasium roof. At times because of these acrobatics, I often thought that we might have been recruited into Billy Smart's Circus instead of the army. We could all do a complete somersault from a standing position and land back on our feet. Physical exercise was also a favourite punishment dealt out by our instructors and twenty or thirty extra push ups was to be expected at least twice a day on the command, "Give me twenty!"

After a few weeks of this we all became quite immune to it and it all seemed to be part of a normal day, we never to cross our instructors. Exercise was quite painful at times especially after you had just been to the medical centre for an injection. Injections were a regular occurrence here, I must have been immunised against everything from the Black Death to Breathing, every member of our squad felt like pin cushions for the first six weeks. We were lined up like cattle and injected with needles of all sizes, maybe we were going to be sent somewhere exotic, to catch some exotic disease, we never knew. It soon became apparent that everything we did was competitive. We were competing against the other squads to see who would be the best at, drill and sport. Then we were set to compete against each other to see who won the Best Recruit of the squad award, then ultimately the Best Recruit of the intake award. How the intake award was going to work was anyone's guess, our intake was split in two 76B and 76B2 who joined us six weeks after we started. They would never catch up. The best recruit competition caused arguments amongst the separate squad members while the rest caused rivalry between the squads. Number two squad of which I was a member never won anything against our rivals, and I won the best recruit award for our squad. I don't know how but it was also me who won the Best Recruit Award for the intake, or should I say two intakes and was rewarded by our members by being thrown into one of the sceptic water tanks beside the bunkers which we ran over. But this all happened as we ended our thirteen weeks in Junior Company.

To fill in the time between getting drilled on parade and running through fields, getting heat exhaustion by orienteering and learning other military tasks like map reading and firing weapons, we had classroom work which we had to carry out to pass our General Engineering Exams. These classroom lessons consisted of welding, metalwork, blacksmithing and soldering wires together along with educational lessons including mathematics, physics and engineering drawing. This all came within the first weeks of our lives at this college. It never rained during this time, forest fires started to break out and the temperature never dropped below seventy degrees, we were cooked throughout the whole of this stage of our training. As we came to the end of our term in junior company and we looked forward to joining our senior companies for our last year or so, it started to rain. It was for one day and a heavy shower, it happened on a weekend and once it started, everyone got into their shorts and ran out onto the parade ground half naked and danced about in the wet stuff from the skies. Steam rose from everywhere, the square, and the bodies of everyone in the rain.

One other thing which was compulsory in junior company was the fact that everyone had to take up a hobby and attend it every Tuesday night for an hour. I decided to join the pipe band as a drummer, hoorah I got my drum at last. For the rest of my stay at the college I was going to be known as a Bandy, not because of my legs either. There were other hobbies I could have taken up, but I quite fancied joining the band, I loved the sound of the bagpipes. I found playing the side drum came very easily to me and improved very quickly. The only problem with being in the band and junior company was the fact you could not go on parade with them until you joined your senior company which only happened after you passed out of your basic training. Basic training was nearly over after you had been on your first tactical camp with them. This was where we were taken out into the middle of no where told to dig a trench and live in it for a week while carrying out patrols attacking make believe enemies and being attacked. This tested us on all of our military skills from map reading to dismantling and cleaning our weapons. We were given a firepower display to show us the effects of blank ammunition, thunder flashes, smoke grenades and trip flares. We were taught to strip and assemble our weapons blindfolded in a certain amount of seconds, why? I will never know. Why would you strip down a weapon, clean it then rebuild it ready to fire if you couldn't see what you were doing. If you couldn't see then how were you meant to be able to shoot someone or something? The staff didn't leave us alone here either and we were often woken up in the middle of the night by a thunder flash being tossed into your trench. When this happened, you grabbed your poncho and got out as quickly as possible, you never left anything in the trench, if you did, you would spend the rest of your life looking for whatever it was you left behind. This final exercise ended with a trip to Pirbright Assault Course.

The assault course was in the middle of a wood in Pirbright, the Guards training depot. We had to work together in our teams to complete it and our team did very well until the twelve foot wall came. I acted as the lift to get my team members up onto the wall and they all went up. The last two were supposed to stay on the wall to help me as the last man over, so once I had helped the last of my team up, I turned to run and get up the wall only to see that my team members had gone. In their eagerness they forgot about me to continue the race against the other squad. There was I staring at this wall wondering what to do and mad at what they had done. I gritted my teeth and ran at the wall, stepped on it to give myself a push and somehow managed to get my fingers on the top of it. Hanging there I started kicking my legs until after what seemed ages managed to get a better grip on the wall and pull myself up. I threw myself off the other side and ran like a lunatic to catch my squad. At the end we were told that our attempts at the assault course had been filmed and we would see it upon returning to camp. We were all too knackered to care, just pleased that we had finished it. When I saw the film, I was embarrassed as they had caught me on the twelve foot wall kicking like a four legged spider on heat trying to scale its height.

Next was our passing out parade, this symbolised the end of basic training and joining our senior companies. Mum turned up to watch and was given the attention normally bestowed upon the queen, and all because I won the best recruit award for my squad and the two intakes. She was proud as punch as she watched me get my award during the parade. We were all sweating buckets and I was blinded by the beads of sweat running down my face, at one stage I thought I might need a snorkel. I was very surprised that no one passed out (fainted) on this parade. It would have given a different meaning to the whole event. It was a couple of days after this that we were moved out of junior block and to our senior company spiders, where we all thought that life would only be a lot better. Time would tell, we went on leave for a short time after this only for me to return to B Company spider and all it had in store for me.

Chapter 5

Senior Company (B Coy)

OK so I left Junior Company in 1976, now I had two years in B Company where I was to finish my apprenticeship before being shipped out into the big wild world.

I'm middle row third from the left this time, and yes the sun is still shining!

Senior Company (B Coy)

OK so I left Junior Company and was now a member of B Company, my senior company for the remaining time I spent at the Army Apprentices College. This was a little like jumping out of the frying pan and into the fire to start with, we were all used to being bullied and picked on by our initial instructors, but when it moved on to where your other apprentices who had been there longer picking on you, it started to become ridiculous. This was where I worked out my own methods and tactics to deal with this, much to the surprise of a lot of people, but it seemed to work. Firstly, always plead ignorant, in other words act thick and insist on a demonstration of what anyone wants you to do so that you can carry out their demands correctly. Secondly always agree with them, so if they call you an idiot, tell them that they are right and that you are the biggest idiot you know, this works a treat, thirdly if they give you something to do always ask if you can do something else for them at the same time to make your life harder, this confuses people and finally always keep a smile on your face, this annoys them, because they are trying to get you mad, but if you smile at them all the time and put on a happy face, it makes them get mad and eventually they will give up on you and go to annoy some easier prey.

There was one occasion while I was on cookhouse duty where I had to sweep and mop the kitchen floor, I was busy mopping away when one of the lads came up to me and told me to do it properly. I told him I was doing it properly, when he insisted that I was not, I stopped and asked him how. He spent five minutes explaining to me how to mop a floor, when he finished, I continued my task the same way as I started. He watched me for a minute and clearly frustrated by me washing the floor in the same manner demanded the mop from me and ordered me to watch him. I watched him demonstrate how to mop a floor, then, he asked me if I understood. I told him I wasn't quite sure and asked him to show me again which he promptly did. This went on two or three times and he had mopped most of the floor before he realised that I was winding him up. He handed me the mop back and stormed off in frustration. He never questioned how I did things again after that. I put the mop and bucket away admiring my nicely mopped floor.

Cookhouse duties and guard duties were just two of the regular extra jobs which had to be done on top of our normal work, but if you were sensible, these could be quite easy to carry out without too much effort. Guard duty meant you went on parade at six in the evening at the barracks guardroom and you had to take it in turns to patrol the camp or man the barrier at the main entrance. During guard duty, you worked for two hours, then you had four hours off, but you could not leave the guardroom during your four hours off, so you utilised this time by sleeping. As you were promoted, you then became either second in command of the guard or guard commander. As guard commander, you did not have to patrol or man the gate, but you were responsible for ensuring that the guard rota was carried out properly, which meant all the guard members were patrolling or sleeping at the correct times, this meant that as guard commander, you got less sleep. Cookhouse duty was not spud bashing, but cleaning up the kitchens after the cooks while they were working and after they had finished, out of the two duties I must say, I preferred guard duty, this was probably just as well as I seemed to get a lot of them as extra duties in form of punishments. Me and extra duties were to be my hallmark throughout my army career, in fact if I hadn't left the army when I did I would probably still be doing them to this day trying to catch up.

In the senior companies, the competitive streak was kept going by everyone, but now it was against the other companies and not against squads. Each company had its own colour, A company was blue, B company red, C company green and D company was yellow. We played every type of sport against each other and yes I was always picked to play rugby for B company, I later went on to play for the School of Electrical Engineering which was where I was going after leaving the Apprentices College. Our education continued with a variety of practical tests and exams to make sure that everything they were cramming into our heads was staying there. Every morning we had muster parade, where we were inspected, and then we had to report to our groups for our daily work. Weekends and some evenings saw me at band practice and passing out parade rehearsals every Saturday morning. At least I could now play in the band and soon gained recognition. When the lead drummer of the pipe band left the college, I took his place and was soon promoted to the rank of junior Lance Corporal.

Every term we had to go on outward bound training, this was where we were all taught to walk for miles across somewhere like Dartmoor or up mountains like Snowden. After walking up Snowden via a sheer drop known as the knife edge, passing through the clouds and freezing to bits to reach the top, we were informed that there was a train that would have took us up there, but only officers were allowed to travel that way. We thought we might get a lift back to the bottom, but no, we had to walk back. These camps were used to get us wet in canoes, where every lesson started with a capsize drill. We were taught to sail dinghy's abseil backwards off cliff faces, normally with a slightly short rope, rock climb up mountains with walls like a sheet of glass and pothole. Potholing consisted of crawling around in a damp, wet, dark hole in the ground with a torch like thing strapped to your head. These were fun days especially for the instructors. At least it got us out of the camp for a week. The fitness tests kept coming along with the parades and duties, we all eagerly read orders every morning, these were instructions written on a piece of A4 paper by someone sitting in an office giving us our instructions for the day.

It paid you to keep on the right side of everyone while you were in the companies, otherwise you could end up locked in a steel locker, or your gear which consisted of your steel locker, bedside cabinet, bedside mat and bed with you in it could be moved in the middle of the night to the middle of the parade square. Can you imagine waking up there just as everyone was going on parade at six o clock in the morning? That was how you found out who was not fitting in too well with everyone else.

Being in the band was not always plain sailing. I soon discovered that we had to carry out public parades at weekends as well as normal parades and practices during the week. It wasn't long before I was promoted again to Drum Major of the pipe band and was to become the senior Drum Major of all three of the college's bands. I was also promoted to Junior Corporal closely followed by promotion to Sergeant. I was then Platoon Sergeant for the band section of B Company. The Company Sergeant Major decided that it would be a good idea to put all of the companies' band members into one platoon of the company, with me in charge of them. This went down well with all the band members. I had my own room at this time and was responsible for all of their activities. This did not go down well with some the other non band platoons, especially when I had to take their morning parades, following the rotas set out in the company orders. No one understood my rank as I was the only one who wore four upside down stripes with a drum above them on my right sleeve, normal sergeants only wore the three stripes. It took a few months for everyone to get used to this, including the permanent staff. Being in this position, I had to be a little harder on the men I was in charge of, because band members were thought of by non band members to be inferior to the rest of the men. Their idea was that because they carried weapons on their passing out parades and band members didn't, they were bigger and tougher than us. Silly I thought, because we also knew rifle drill and could carry it out to the same standard as them, but we had our instruments to carry on parades, where were we meant to put a rifle, up our kilts? The bayonet was too sharp!

Every term as a band on the morning of the passing out parade, the whole college was woken up by the band marching in a disorderly fashion around the camp playing Black Bear, a Scottish tune. This was the only time we were allowed to play it, we never played it on parades. This always seemed to disgruntle everybody else on the camp, probably because this tradition was not made by the permanent staff or published on our weekly orders. It was the band getting their own back for the jokes played on them during each and every term. Weekend displays were great at times and trying at other times. We were sent to do a charity display at a mental hospital once when one of the tenants decided to follow me on parade. He marched behind me for the whole display, much to the amusement of our audience, I had to be careful with my signals to the band using my mace and kept listening to him ask if he could play a drum when we had finished. It was near the end of the display when he started asking what we wore under our kilts, then decided as we marched off to lift the back of my kilt to show everyone what we wore, but because he lifted the back of the kilt, nothing came to light as he was lifting it all the other pleats fell into place keeping everything covered. At the end of the display, everyone fell about laughing and our embarrassed permanent staff pipe major commended me for not swiping him with my mace and keeping a cool head. He didn't know what I was thinking of doing as he followed me about. This display was the best reception that we ever received anywhere.

The Junior Band Competition was drawing ever nearer, we had never won it, it had always been won by the Royal Corps of Transport Corps of Drums. This meant we were all determined to win this competition for once. Every chance we got the band was out rehearsing their music and display drills. Finally the competition came and judges appeared from everywhere, the strange thing was the fact that each band was judged in their own barracks, so rival bands never met. I was the senior band member at this time as Drum Major of the Pipe Band and led the whole parade. Photographs were taken of us as we marched around our deserted parade ground and when we finished, we all felt that we could do no more. This was my final term at the college and would leave to go up the road to the School of Electronic Engineering to finish my trade training. The results would come after I had left.

Everyone at the college was into motorbikes, except for a few motor mechanics which had passed their tests and bought cars. I had bought a Yamaha RD 200 motorbike which I loved. It took me a little time to get my confidence up on it, but I soon settled down. I had all the gear, leather jacket, boots and full face helmet, I felt great when I was out on my orange machine. I used to go out most evenings to get something from the local chip shop or just to ride about. I kept this bike for about six months until I left the School of Electronic Engineering.

Passing out parade from the college was fast approaching and we were all looking forward to moving on to our next phase of training at the higher colleges, but I was informed that my mum and dad could not make it. Never mind, on the day it was just like every other passing out parade for me, the junior RSM ordered everyone to Get On Parade!. I started the whole thing off getting the parade started by bellowing out my usual order, Band Pipes and Drums, Get On. PARADE! I gave the salute on the final march past and as soon as it started it was all over. This was where I hung up my kilt and mace for the next Drum Major to take over.

The following day everyone went on leave only to return in two weeks to their new colleges. Mine was about five minutes away from this college, Vehicle Mechanics went to Bordon and Aircraft Technicians went to Middle Wallop. This was farewell to the Army Apprentices College for us, leaving behind some good and even more, bad memories.

Chapter 6

Trade Training

Trade Training was done at our Higher Colleges.

My Higher College was the School of Electronic Engineering. Yes you guessed, it was still at Arborfield.

Happy Days!!!

Trade Training

So now I had left the Apprentices College and everyone was now at their Higher Colleges for what the army called Trade Training. My college was about five minutes up the road from the one I had just left. Never mind I still had my trusted Yamaha motorbike.

Family events that took place during my time at the Army Apprentices college were, Steve, my oldest brother had bought his first two flats which were originally one house, but had been converted by someone earlier these cost about two hundred pounds each. I spent a lot of my time on leave helping him to put them right. Bobby had left the army and was working at Vickers, mum and dad were still living in Newburn, Christine was working in a sewing factory on Scotswood Road and my youngest sisters were at school. Steve got married while I was at the Army Apprentices College and apart from my two weddings later on in life his was the only family wedding I got to attend. He married a woman called Bernie and they had three kids together, Andrea, Lee and Jamie. This meant that I was now an uncle with one niece and two nephews. Steve was still working at Throckley Brickworks.

Back at the School of Electronic Engineering, I was roped into playing rugby, so nothing changed there. There was a disco inside the camp on a Friday, where the local girls were invited, so we all got dressed up in our glad rags and went there, but instead of us picking up the lasses, we all generally just ended up in a drunken stupor. We also went out at weekends sometimes to Reading for the night life this was where we learned to watch our backs. Although Reading and Arborfield are well known for the military people in the area, there was also another breed of local people there who the military personnel got to know and name, squaddie bashers. These were gangs of young blokes who had nothing better to do but go out at weekends and target military people to fight with. On one occasion three of us got jumped on by a gang, I hit the floor and was getting kicked while the other two ran away. Luckily, there was an old lady passing by and the lads ran off when she approached, she asked me what had happened and when I told her, she told me off and pointed me in the direction of the bus stop. Upon my arrival back at camp, one of my friends was already back and asked where the other one was. We soon discovered that the other one, who arrived back half an hour later had run the whole nine miles back to camp, we all had a good laugh about this afterwards especially at my running friends' expense. On another occasion I was out at the local pub when a fight broke out between me and another soldier, I had been drinking and went to punch him, but he ducked and I hit a brick wall dislocating two knuckles in my right hand. I didn't realise they were dislocated at the time and thought they were only bruised, it wasn't until the swelling went down that my right hand looked wrong, they have been dislocated ever since and even today, I can still show people where my knuckles are and where they should be.

Anyway back to trade training, why it was called trade training I could never work out. What had I been doing for the past two year or so? I got my City and Guilds results, I took three exams, these were electronic principles A. mathematics A and telecommunications A. With my past history I was surprised at the result I achieved a Distinction a Credit and a Pass. Believe it or not the distinction was in maths. This was the first mathematics exam I had ever passed first time. At this time I also received an award for best achievement from the Apprentices College, I was on a roll. Then I heard the news that in the Junior Bands Competition, we won and I was supposed to rejoin the band to collect the prize on their behalf, I was quite excited about this, but guess what! It never happened and the new Drum Major took all the credit. Still I was enjoying myself at the weekend parties and being taught on the real equipment which I would be working on in my first posting, or so I thought. I was to be posted to Celle in Germany home to the army locating regiment, which had specialist equipment not included on this course I was taking. When I addressed this problem, I was told not to worry as I was to do another six week course six weeks after finishing the course I was on already. Yes I had an extra three month after everyone else was sent out into the big wide world. I began to think that my service time would be up before I left the training establishments of Arborfield.

Back at home my other brother Bobby had bought his first house in Lemington and was busy refurbishing it with a little help from the family, including me while I was on leave. He decided that the ceiling in his living room needed replacing along with the joists which supported the upstairs bedroom floor. We set about removing this and only had the joists to remove, after loosening everything off, Bobby decided it was time to drop the floor. He came upstairs and started loosening the ties holding it up, once this was done, the floor stayed where it was. Protecting the downstairs fire surround with planks of wood, he returned to the upstairs where he decided again to try and drop the floor. He climbed onto the upstairs fire surrounds' hearth and hit it with some force as I stood by the bedroom floor. The ceiling and floor dropped in a loud crash kicking up a dust cloud which we were lost in, success at last. Once the dust settled, we realised that it had broken the downstairs protective timbers, damaging the fireplace and causing a mountain of debris. Not only that, when I looked in the room where Bobby was to check that he hadn't gone down with the floor, I noticed him sitting on the fireplace in the middle of an upstairs room with no floor. For Bobby to get out, he had two choices, either drop onto the rubble below, or attempt to jump over to the doorway where I stood. Once I had stopped laughing, we decided that the safest bet was for him to lower himself downstairs, while I cleared a space so we could open the door and let him out. We were great odd job men. Every job we turned our hands to had an odd ending!

On my way home for this leave period, I had decided to bring my motorbike home, but instead of riding it all the way, I decided to bring it on the train, the whole journey was a disaster making me decide never to do it again. It started when I disembarked at London Charing Cross station and had to make my way across London for my second train. I was riding along behind a taxi when we came up to some traffic lights on red I pulled up, but forgot to put my feet down once I was stationary. This caused me to fall over with the bike in the middle of the road. I managed to pick myself up along with the bike before the lights turned green much to the amusement of passers by and a confused taxi driver who wondered where I had gone from his rear view mirror. Eventually I made my second train which transported me and my motorbike to Newcastle station. Once again I was on my bike driving towards home until I arrived at Scotswood Bridge where a lorry driver in the wrong lane clipped my bikes' rear wheel and headed off over the bridge without stopping or realising what he had done. I on the other hand was knocked off the road onto the grass verge beside the bridge cursing and swearing at the lorry when I noticed that it had not stopped. Eventually when I got home, I got lectures from my parents on how motorbikes were unsafe and I was stupid to buy one, good job I didn't tell them of my eventful journey to come and see them. This was the start of several small accidents on my bike, but the final straw was while I was back at Arborfield and the bike back wheel slipped on the road while it was pouring with rain. The bike bounced off up the road with me following it after jumping off over the back box. The bike stopped by parking itself up a tree was a little bent, so after unbending it a little and repairing the jammed brakes, I took it back to camp and parked it up. I don't think I ever rode that bike again. In fact when I was posted out, I left the keys in it and told everyone that whoever wanted it could have it. I still do not know what happened to it.

During my stay at the School of Electronic Engineering I ended up on guard duty over the Christmas period. It was during one of these duties that we were informed that a suspicious package had been delivered for one of the men. When quizzed about this parcel, the bloke told everyone that he was not expecting a parcel, so the bomb squad were called. They took the package away and blew it up with a controlled explosion. Upon inspection of the remains, they discovered that it was an innocent package intended for the person it was addressed to containing his Christmas presents from home. This cheered us up altogether, but the lad in question was understandably upset, oh well at least he could go home and explain the situation to his family over the New Year.

Trade training continued for three months. We were taught practical and theory on missile guidance systems, gun control loops, artillery computing equipment and infantry radar called Zebedee. No it wasn't from the magic roundabout, but should probably have been put to bed years earlier. I was now playing rugby for the school as long as I hadn't gained an extra duty for some misdemeanour I had done. This place taught electronics to armies from all over the world, there were Africans, Iranians and Iraqis on this camp and I remember that when things were going wrong in their home countries, they would just walk out of lessons switch on the television and watch the news to see if they could return home. All training for these visitors was treated as attendance courses. As long as they turned up they would end up qualified. We on the other hand were subjected to tests and exams on all subjects to pass the course. Eventually we all passed were promoted to Lance Corporal and sent out to our new postings. That is everyone except me. I was put onto the staffing lists at the school and spent six weeks repairing the training rigs. I gained extra knowledge and experience on the equipment all of which would be of no use to me on my first posting. Six weeks of this, then I was introduced to my instructor who was brought in especially for the course to commence my trade training on the specialist equipment I would be working on when I arrived at my first posting in Germany.

The AN/USD 501 Drone system was not one piece of equipment, but a mixture of about ten. It had programmers, cameras of which there were two types, high pressure pneumatic units, launchers, recovery vehicles, recovery beacons and photograph developing and interpretation kit. Where was I to start? I discovered after six weeks of this course that there was another course which just dealt with the cameras, but I completed that course later in my career. Everything was initials like, ULTE, HPPU, T and R, and PPIV. You had to stay on top of everything to keep up with what was going on, this continued all the time you were working with this equipment. I also discovered that everyone was also part of something else like the FRT (Forward Repair Team). I started to think that things did not exist unless it had a daft abbreviation. I was taught to test every piece of equipment, fault find and program. By the time this six week course was over, I knew everything about it, including the names of the REME personnel who worked on it. It was at this time that I discovered that there were only four locating batteries in the whole British army who operated this equipment. Three in Celle Germany and one in Larkhill, I would serve with them all, so I was eventually known by everyone working with the locating regiments and not just because of my antics while off duty, but for my skills at testing the programmer modules of the system. I became known as the programmer king. Upon completion of this course, I was posted out to Germany, but the story from here will continue in my next book, The Ramblings of a Geordie (Part 2).

Chapter 7

Changes So Far

From This…

As was mentioned earlier in this book, it is not just about what I've been up to, but to highlight some of the changes that I have noticed from then until now.

Here is the list so far, see how many things you can remember!

Changes So Far

OK so here we go with changes and memories that have occurred so far during my life up to being at the School of Electronic Engineering, let's start with the year I was born. I was born in September nineteen fifty nine a day or so before Buddy Holly and the Big Bopper were killed in an air crash. The coal slag heap at Newburn still had a rounded top on it and everyone spent money in pounds, shillings and pence, the smallest legal currency I can remember is one half penny in old money. There were twelve pennies in a shilling and a half crown was two shillings and sixpence. Television was just about to become popular and was only in black and white, you used to change channels with a rotary switch on the wall provided by a company called Redifusion. Everyone watched football, before money spoilt the game and adults spent their weekends at the local working mans clubs.

Newburn Fire Station was still operational, Scotswood used to have houses running down the hill towards Scotswood Road, The Robin Adair public house was still standing and the Newburn Riverside park was still a little wild and unkempt. The drill hall at Newburn was used as the army cadet training establishment and the local boys club. Armstrong's Factory was still on Scotswood Road and Spencers' Spring Factory was on Walbottle Road. The Beatles were one of the newest and most popular groups around and your parents could buy single cigarettes at the shop, they could even buy them in packets of five. We all used to play football in the streets and police would give you a clip around the ear if you were caught doing something wrong.

The railway bridge at Newburn was still standing and the rag and bone man would come around on a horse and cart to collect your unwanted items and reward the kids with a balloon. Sunday mornings were spent at the Newcastle Quayside Market the place to buy your bargains and most kids had short back and side's haircuts. Who remembers watching Watch with Mother on the TV? There was Muffin the Mule, the Wooden Tops and Bill and Ben. You bought sweets from the shops and sometimes you were given a lucky bag. As kids we played conkers which fell from the local trees and we hardened with vinegar. We played Cowboys and Indians as well as Cops and Robbers. Sometimes we dressed up and pretended we were superheroes. There were pogo sticks and stilts, roller skates and bikes. A popular bike we had as kids was the Raleigh Chopper bike with big handle bars and gears.

If you remember the song 'Blaydon Races', you will notice why it could not be written these days. Here are some of the reasons why.
'We got the bus from Balmra's'
Balmra's bus station was renamed Marleborough, and now it is no longer there, it is the Centre for Life, a new modern building. Next part of the song included,
'We flew past Armstrongs Factory
And up to the Robin Adair.
Just gannin doon the railway bridge,
The bus wheel flew off there.'
Armstrongs factory became Mitchel Bearings and Vickers, but is now known as BAE. The Robin Adair was pulled down and now has a garage on its site and the railway bridge at Newburn is no longer there, it too was demolished.

The fire station at Newburn is now a bicycle shop and the houses in Scotswood are now flattened. A lot of the houses in Throckley have been re modernised, changing the character of the area, all the playground areas have vanished and the kids play in the streets. The riverside has been redeveloped and tidied up and new industrial estates have been built in Throckley and Newburn.

The Centurion Public house in Throckley is now a new care home and Andy Bartons Garage at Newburn is now owned by someone else. There used to be juvenile jazz bands throughout the area, how many of you can remember, Throckley High Fliers, The Newburnaires, The Red Arrows, Gosforth Gunners, Lemington Globetrotters and Blucher Blutonions. I bet you have heard of them if you are from the area if not a member youselves.

There were memorial parades down Newburn Road to the monument every remembrance Sunday which woke everyone up to take place in the two minute silence. Everyone knew everyone else and there was a great sense of community spirit. There were Grammar Schools and Secondary Schools, now they are all Comprehensive Schools. Corporal punishment was allowed in schools and we were brought up to fend for ourselves. Work was hard to come by, but everyone wanted to work and found ways to get money and survive without breaking into houses. Who remembers Triumph Herald cars, taking bottles back to the shops for the money back on them, going blackberry picking, potato picking and travelling up the road to pick your own strawberries? Mum used to bake every weekend to feed us and every weekend we would clear the plates. At school you were taught road safety by Tufty the squirrel and at Christmas we used to make our own decorations. Treats for us was being taken to the cinema in Newcastle to watch films like Snow White and the Seven Dwarfs or Bed knobs and Broomsticks where we were always bought sweets to eat during the film. The lyric at Throckley used to be a picture hall before it was partly demolished and is now an off license. The co op shop was built and is now a Sainsbury's.

Toys we all used to play with were Action Men, Girls played with Sindy and her little sister Patch, who remembers building their own cart with pieces of wood and wheels from old broken prams? Liquorice was a favourite sweet in the shape of bootlaces, there was lumpy mashed potato with school dinners and puddings made from semolina and figs. Everyone remembers Woolworths and the packets of Pick and Mix that grandmothers and mothers brought home after their shopping trips in town.

There were Hot Pants and Flares along with platform boots and shoes in the fashion, tank tops and shirts with wide collars in very bright colours were also worn in abundance. Glam Rock hit the charts in the seventies, this was later replaced with Punk Rock from a strange group of people who liked to pierce their bodies with strange items such as safety pins. These punk rockers were very angry anti establishment bodies who had a lot of records banned.

Then there was the miners strikes, fireman strikes and power company strikes for better pay and conditions. The miners strikes were very memorable as Newcastle was predominantly a mining area. It was during these strikes the communities began to pull together again. There was Friday nights out at the local club to play bingo and if you won, you thought that you had won the lottery.

There has been lots of changes so far and there will be many more to come. All of the family is now married either for the first or second time, kids hang about in the streets with nothing to do, all the places of entertainment are slowly disappearing, so perhaps some future changes might put things right and help to rebuild the community that was.

Changes So Far

...To This

OK! So I have gone from short pants to a kilt.

How many other changes do you remember?

www.ingramcontent.com/pod-product-compliance
Lightning Source LLC
LaVergne TN
LVHW091239150826
845673LV00003B/1213

* 9 7 8 1 4 4 7 7 9 4 2 9 5 *